THE LITTLE RED BOOK OF

HOPE

THE LITTLE RED BOOK OF
HOPE

Edited by Nick Lyons and Tony Lyons

Skyhorse Publishing

Skyhorse Publishing books may be purchased in bulk at special discounts
for sales promotion, corporate gifts, fund-raising, or educational purposes.
Special editions can also be created to specifications. For details, contact
the Special Sales Department, Skyhorse Publishing,
307 West 36th Street, 11th Floor, New York, NY 10018 or
info@skyhorsepublishing.com.

Skyhorse® and Skyhorse Publishing® are registered trademarks of
Skyhorse Publishing, Inc.®, a Delaware corporation.

Visit our website at www.skyhorsepublishing.com.

10 9 8 7 6 5 4 3 2 1

Library of Congress Cataloging-in-Publication Data

Lyons, Nick.
  The little red book of hope / Nick Lyons and Tony Lyons.
    pages cm
  ISBN 978-1-62087-559-9 (alk. paper)
1. Hope—Quotations, maxims, etc. 2. Conduct of life—Quotations,
maxims, etc. I. Title.
  PN6084.H62L96 2013
  081—dc23

                        2012049525

Printed in China

For Lina

Contents

Introduction

Hope takes a thousand different forms. It can be as simple as a young child wishing for a birthday present or as broad and global as a conscious desire for more peace in a world that desperately needs more people bridging the sometimes vast differences between nations and cultures.

Hope can be personal, political, religious, local, international, or, connected to the outcome of a life or love or a sports event or a lottery. A number of the authors in this book strongly note the differences between the "hope" that is possible, that is rooted in one's own abilities to affect the outcome, and the hope that is related to mere chance.

Hope can animate challenge and invigorate a life and sometimes lead to false hopes or even delusions. You'll find these and many more examples of hopes in this little collection, as well as a few examples that resist fitting into any category. All, we hope, will help you understand this universal activity of the human mind more wisely.

—Nick Lyons and Tony Lyons

1

Growing Up

Never let go of hope. One day you will see that it all has finally
come together. What you have always wished for has finally come
to be. You will look back and laugh at what has passed and you
will ask yourself. . . "How did I get through all of that?"
—Anonymous

• • •

Young people have an almost biological destiny to be hopeful.
—Marshall Ganz

• • •

Listen to the mustn'ts, child. Listen to the don'ts. Listen to the shouldn'ts, the impossibles, the won'ts. Listen to the never haves, then listen close to me. . . . Anything can happen, child. Anything can be.
—SHEL SILVERSTEIN

• • •

Maybe everyone can live beyond what they're capable of.
—MARKUS ZUSAK, *I AM THE MESSENGER*

• • •

A baby is God's opinion that the world should go on.
—CARL SANDBURG

• • •

It's the children the world almost breaks who grow up to save it.
—FRANK WARREN

• • •

We pass through this world but once. Few tragedies can be more extensive than the stunting of life, few injustices deeper than the denial of an opportunity to strive or even to hope, by a limit imposed from without, but falsely identified as lying within.
—STEPHEN JAY GOULD, *THE MISMEASURE OF MAN*

• • •

With every mistake, we must surely be learning.
—GEORGE HARRISON

• • •

The first duty of a man is to think for himself.
—JOSÉ MARTÍ

• • •

I'm inspired by the love people have for their children. And I'm inspired by my own children, how full they make my heart. They make me want to work to make the world a little bit better. And they make me want to be a better man.
—BARACK OBAMA

• • •

Then you must teach my daughter this same lesson. How to lose your innocence but not your hope. How to laugh forever.
—AMY TAN, *THE JOY LUCK CLUB*

• • •

in a woman's womb.
another chance.
to make the world better.
—ELLEN HOPKINS, *BURNED*

• • •

Hopes are like hair ornaments. Girls want to wear too many of them. When they become old women they look silly wearing even one.
—ARTHUR GOLDEN, *MEMOIRS OF A GEISHA*

• • •

Ask yourself these three questions, Tatiana Metanova, and you will know who you are. Ask: What do believe in? What do you hope for? What do you love?
—PAULLINA SIMONS, *THE BRONZE HORSEMAN*

• • •

Have you ever hoped for something? And held out for it against all the odds? Until everything you did was ridiculous?
—ALI SHAW, *THE GIRL WITH GLASS FEET*

• • •

I am not what I ought to be, I am not what I want to be, I am not what I hope to be in another world; but still I am not what I once used to be, and by the grace of God I am what I am.
—JOHN NEWTON

• • •

We never know when our last day on Earth will be. So, love with full sincerity, believe with true faith, and hope with all of your might. Better to have lived in truth and discovered life than to have lived half-heartedly and died long before you ever ceased breathing.
—CRISTINA MARRERO

• • •

We all give up great expectations along the way.
—CARLOS RUIZ ZAFÓN, THE ANGEL'S GAME

• • •

An extraterrestrial being, newly arrived on Earth—scrutinizing what we mainly present to our children in television, radio, movies, newspapers, magazines, the comics, and many books—might easily conclude that we are intent on teaching them murder, rape, cruelty, superstition, credulity, and consumerism... What kind of society could we create if, instead, we drummed into them science and a sense of hope?
—CARL SAGAN, THE DEMON-HAUNTED WORLD: SCIENCE AS A CANDLE IN THE DARK

• • •

Time has taught me not to lose hope, yet not to trust too much in hope either.
—CARLOS RUIZ ZAFÓN

• • •

Fairy tales do not tell children that dragons exist. Children already know that dragons exist. Fairy tales tell children that dragons can be killed.
—G. K. Chesterton

• • •

Imagine that you are more than nothing. Evil made you, but you are no more evil than a child unborn. If you want, if you seek, if you hope, who is to say that your hope might not be answered?
—Dean Koontz, *Dead and Alive*

• • •

I hope suffering don't exist.
—David Levithan, *Dash & Lily's Book of Dares*

• • •

Let the children have their night of fun and laughter. Let the gifts of Father Christmas delight their play. Let us grown-ups share to the full in their unstinted pleasures before we turn again to the stern task and the formidable years that lie before us, resolved that, by our sacrifice and daring, these same children shall not be robbed of their inheritance or denied their right to live in a free and decent world.
—Winston Churchill Christmas Eve Message, 1941, As Quoted in *In the Dark Streets Shineth*, David McCullough

• • •

There I was, waiting, afraid I'd never experience the kind of joy
yet to come, but hoping for it just the same.
—ELIZABETH BERG, *THE YEAR OF PLEASURES*

• • •

The thought of our past years in me doth breed
Perpetual benediction: not indeed
For that which is most worthy to be blest—
Delight and liberty, the simple creed
Of Childhood, whether busy or at rest,
With new-fledged hope still fluttering in his breast.
—WILLIAM WORDSWORTH

• • •

Your emotional state has a tremendous amount to do with
sickness, health, and well-being. For years, my husband and I
lived on—and because of—hope. Hope continues to give me the
mental strength to carry on.
—DANA REEVE

• • •

Until we lose ourselves there is no hope of finding ourselves.
—HENRY MILLER

• • •

Hope is a seed that grows inside us from the moment we are born.
—J. D. WILLD

• • •

He had that sense, or inward prophecy,—which a young man had better never have been born than not to have, and a mature man had better die at once than utterly to relinquish,—that we are not doomed to creep on forever in the old bad way, but that, this very now, there are harbingers abroad of a golden era, to be accomplished in his own lifetime.
—NATHANIEL HAWTHORNE, *The House of the Seven Gables*

• • •

Hope is the last thing that dies.
Maybe because hope is one of those dratted things that is truly, honestly, genuinely immortal.
—VERA NAZARIAN, *The Perpetual Calendar of Inspiration*

• • •

Death is more merciful than hope itself! There is nothing surprising in this, for death is divinely appointed, while hope is the creation of human folly. Both end in frustration. Am I destined to lead a life of endless frustration?
—NAGUIB MAHFOUZ, *The Beginning and the End*

• • •

I, now thirty-seven years old in perfect health begin,
Hoping to cease not till Death.
—WALT WHITMAN, *SONG OF MYSELF*

• • •

Woe is the man whose heart has not learned while young to
hope, to love, and to put trust in life.
—JOSEPH CONRAD

• • •

Man wants to live but it is useless to hope that this will dictate all
of his actions.
—ALBERT CAMUS

• • •

Sometimes at dusk, when you were trying to relax and not
think of the general stagnation, the Garbage God would gather
a handful of those choked-off morning hopes and dangle them
somewhere just out of reach; they would hang in the breeze and
make a sound like delicate glass bells, reminding you of
something you never quite got hold of, and never would.
—HUNTER S. THOMPSON

• • •

I hope you live a life you are proud of. If you find that you're not, I hope you have the strength to start all over again.
—F. SCOTT FITZGERALD

• • •

How wrong Emily Dickinson was! Hope is not "the thing with feathers." The thing with feathers has turned out to be my nephew. I must take him to a specialist in Zurich.
—WOODY ALLEN

• • •

She thought it would be detestable to be afraid or ashamed. She had an infinite hope that she would never do anything wrong.
—HENRY JAMES

• • •

. . . in my best dreams I see the day when I shall stand and greet myself.
—RANIER MARIA RILKE

• • •

Life is what happens while you're busy making other plans.
—JOHN LENNON

• • •

The youth have hope because it's their future they're hopeful about and if they're depressed about their own future, well, then we are in a bad state. And we keep hope alive by keeping it alive amongst ourselves.
—JOHN LENNON

• • •

I think it's a mistake to ever look for hope outside of one's self.
—ARTHUR MILLER

• • •

We all hope. It's what keeps us alive.
—DAVID MAMET

• • •

Today's students can put dope in their veins or hope in their brains.
—Jesse Jackson

● ● ●

Middle age is when you're sitting at home on a Saturday night and the telephone rings and you hope it isn't for you.
—Ogden Nash

● ● ●

Youth is easily deceived because it is quick to hope.
—Aristotle

● ● ●

To help the young soul, to add energy, inspire hope, and blow the coals into a useful flame; to redeem defeat by new thought and firm action, this, though not easy, is the work of divine man.
—Ralph Waldo Emerson

● ● ●

2

The World Around Us

I still believe in Hope—mostly because there's no such place as
Fingers Crossed, Arkansas.
—MOLLY IVINS

• • •

History is moving, and it will tend toward hope, or tend toward
tragedy.
—GEORGE W. BUSH

• • •

To travel hopefully is a better thing than to arrive.
—ROBERT LOUIS STEVENSON

• • •

The past is a source of knowledge, and the future is a source of hope. Love of the past implies faith in the future.
—Stephen Ambrose, *Fast Company*

• • •

You can cut all the flowers but you cannot keep Spring from coming.
—Pablo Neruda

• • •

I don't think of all the misery, but of the beauty that still remains.
—Anne Frank, *The Diary of a Young Girl*

• • •

Half of the American people have never read a newspaper. Half never voted for President. One hopes it is the same half.
—Gore Vidal

• • •

The thing the sixties did was to show us the possibilities and the responsibility that we all had. It wasn't the answer. It just gave us a glimpse of the possibility.
—JOHN LENNON

• • •

We carry within us the wonders we seek without us.
—THOMAS BROWNE

• • •

Though nothing can bring back the hour
Of splendor in the grass, of glory in the flower;
We will grieve not, rather find
Strength in what remains behind;
In the primal sympathy
Which having been must ever be . . .
—WILLIAM WORDSWORTH

• • •

Shoot for the moon, and if you miss you'll still be among the stars.
—CECELIA AHERN, *P.S. I Love You*

• • •

And the past held only this wisdom: that love was a damaging mistake, and its accomplice, hope, a treacherous illusion. And whenever those twin poisonous flowers began to sprout in the parched land of that field, Mariam uprooted them.
—Khaled Hosseini, *A Thousand Splendid Suns*

• • •

This is where it all begins. Everything starts here, today.
—David Nicholls, *One Day*

• • •

Come friends, it's not too late to seek a newer world.
—Alfred Lord Tennyson

• • •

Hope is a force of nature. Don't let anyone tell you different.
—Jim Butcher, *Changes*

• • •

Hope and Memory have one daughter and her name is Art, and she has built her dwelling far from the desperate field where men hang out their garments upon forked boughs to be banners of battle. O beloved daughter of Hope and Memory, be with me for a while.
—W. B. YEATS

• • •

Should we continue to look upwards? Is the light we can see in the sky one of those which will presently be extinguished? The ideal is terrifying to behold . . . brilliant but threatened on all sides by the dark forces that surround it: nevertheless, no more in danger than a star in the jaws of the clouds.
—VICTOR HUGO, *LES MISÉRABLES*

• • •

Hope . . . which whispered from Pandora's box after all the other plagues and sorrows had escaped, is the best and last of all things. Without it, there is only time. And time pushes at our backs like a centrifuge, forcing outward and away, until it nudges us into oblivion. . .
—IAN CALDWELL, *THE RULE OF FOUR*

• • •

Andy: Forget that . . . there are places in this world that aren't made out of stone. That there's something inside . . . that they can't get to, that they can't touch. That's yours.
Red: What're you talking about?
Andy: Hope.
—STEPHEN KING, *DIFFERENT SEASONS*

• • •

And the end of all our exploring
Will be to arrive where we started
And know the place for the first time.
—T. S. ELIOT

• • •

In an age of hope men looked up at the night sky and saw "the heavens." In an age of hopelessness they call it simply "space."
—PETER KREEFT

• • •

I'll admit that my garden now grows hope in lavish profusion, leaving little room for anything else. I suppose it has squeezed out more practical plants like caution and common sense. Still, though, hope does not flourish in every garden, and I feel thankful it has taken root in mine.
—SHARON KAY PENMAN, *THE RECKONING*

• • •

One of the gravestones in the cemetery near the earliest church has an anchor on it and an hourglass, and the words "In Hope." Why did they put that above a dead person? Was it the corpse hoping, or those still alive?
—MARGARET ATWOOD, *THE HANDMAID'S TALE*

• • •

We mourn the blossoms of May because they are to whither; but we know that May is one day to have its revenge upon November, by the revolution of that solemn circle which never stops—which teaches us in our height of hope, ever to be sober, and in our depth of desolation, never to despair.
—WILLIAM PETER BLATTY, *THE EXORCIST*

• • •

When hope is fleeting, stop for a moment and visualize, in a sky of silver, the crescent of a lavender moon. Imagine it—delicate, slim, precise, like a paper-thin slice from a cabochon jewel.
It may not be very useful, but it is beautiful.
And sometimes it is enough.
—Vera Nazarian, *The Perpetual Calendar of Inspiration*

• • •

What can I say about life? Do I praise it for letting you live, or damn it for allowing the rest?
—Janet Fitch, *White Oleander*

• • •

I thought: hope cannot be said to exist, nor can it be said not to exist. It is just like roads across the earth. For actually the earth had no roads to begin with, but when many men pass one way, a road is made.
—Lu Hsun

• • •

Each day means a new twenty-four hours. Each day means everything's possible again. You live in the moment, you take it all one day at a time. . . You try to walk in the light.
—Marie Lu

• • •

Are we alone? Over time, you will come up with various answers
to that same nagging question. Eventually one day it will occur to
you that this endless asking is the answer you have been looking
for. The fact that we have an ongoing dialogue with the universe
is proof enough that there is "something" out there.
—VERONIQUE VIENNE, *THE ART OF THE MOMENT: SIMPLE
WAYS TO GET THE MOST FROM LIFE*

• • •

With the need for the self in the time of another /
I left my seaport grim and dear /
knowing good work could be made /
in the state governed by both Hope and Despair.
—ROMAN PAYNE

• • •

The journey through another world, beyond bad dreams
beyond the memories of a murdered generation,
cartographed in captivity by bare survivors
makes sacristans of us all.
—ELIZABETH COOK-LYNN

• • •

Hope is a journey
Into an enchanted tomorrow
—KAREN HACKEL, *THE WHISPER OF YOUR SOUL*

• • •

I thought that the light-house looked lovely as hope,
That star on life's tremulous ocean.
—THOMAS MOORE

• • •

Move on, sky is not limit, wind can touch you, water can dip you,
mother will care you, wife will nurture you and above all, one day
you will see your child following, up above the sky; you became
a star, twinkling, watching and waiting to come back again, on
earth.
—SANTOSH KALWAR

• • •

Let truth be told—women do as a rule live through such
humiliations, and regain their spirits, and again look about them
with an interested eye. While there's life there's hope is a conviction not so entirely unknown to the "betrayed" as some amiable
theorists would have us believe.
—THOMAS HARDY, *TESS OF THE D'URBERVILLES*

• • •

Hope is a straw hat hanging beside a window covered with frost.
—Margaret George, *Mary Queen of Scotland
and the Isles*

• • •

Crime, violence, infamy are not tragedy. Tragedy occurs when a
human soul awakes and seeks, in suffering and pain, to free itself
from crime, violence, infamy, even at the cost of life. The struggle
is the tragedy—not defeat or death. That is why the spectacle of
tragedy has always filled men, not with despair, but with a sense
of hope and exaltation.
—Whittaker Chambers, *Witness*

• • •

"Many are less fortunate than you" may not be a roof to live
under, but it will serve to retire beneath in the event of a shower.
—Georg Christoph Lichtenberg

• • •

I think at the heart of so much restlessness of the day is a spiritual
vacuum. There is a yearning for meaningful lives, a yearning for
values we can commonly embrace. I hear an almost inaudible
but pervasive discontent with the price we pay for our current
materialism. And I hear a fluttering of hope that there might be
more to life than bread and circuses.
—Bill Moyers

• • •

If the single man plants himself indomitably on his instincts, and
there abides, this huge world will come around to him.
—Ralph Waldo Emerson

• • •

There it must be, I think, in the vast and eternal laws of matter,
and not in the daily cares and sins and troubles of men, that
whatever is more than animal within us must find its solace and
its hope. I hope, or I could not live.
—H. G. Wells, *The Island of Dr. Moreau*

• • •

Give me your tired, your poor,
Your huddled masses yearning to breathe free,
The wretched refuse of your teeming shore.
Send these, the homeless, tempest-tost to me,
I lift my lamp beside the golden door!
—Emma Lazarus

• • •

Auspicious Hope! in thy sweet garden grow
Wreaths for each toil, a charm for every woe.
—THOMAS CAMPBELL, *PLEASURES OF HOPE*

• • •

Man is, properly speaking, based upon hope; he has no other
possession but hope; this world of his is emphatically a place of
hope.
—THOMAS CARLYLE

• • •

Man himself has become our greatest hazard and our only hope.
—JOHN STEINBECK

• • •

I hope we shall crush in its birth the aristocracy of our monied
corporations. . .
—THOMAS JEFFERSON

• • •

The truth, the hope of any time, must always be sought in minorities.
—RALPH WALDO EMERSON

• • •

One loves to possess arms though they hope never to have occasion for them.
—THOMAS JEFFERSON

• • •

Our job is to make sure that even as we make progress that we are also giving people a sense of hope and vision for the future.
—BARACK OBAMA

• • •

The world is all gates, all opportunities.
—RALPH WALDO EMERSON

• • •

I hope in these days we have heard the last of conformity and consistency.
—RALPH WALDO EMERSON

• • •

The charm of fishing is that it is the pursuit of what is elusive but attainable, a perpetual series of occasions for hope.
—JOHN BUCHAN

• • •

. . . William Stegner . . . coined the term "the geography of hope," countering the argument that wilderness preservation served elites with the assertion that wilderness could be a place in which everyone could locate their hopefulness even if few actually entered it.
—REBECCA SOLNIT, *STORMING THE GATES OF PARADISE: LANDSCAPES FOR POLITICS*

• • •

3

Joy

They say a person needs just three things to be truly happy in this world: someone to love, something to do, and something to hope for.

—Tom Bodett

• • •

May you have enough happiness to make you sweet, enough trials to make you strong, enough sorrow to keep you human, enough hope to make you happy.

—Anonymous

• • •

Strong hope is a much greater stimulant of life than any realized
joy could be.
—FRIEDRICH NIETZSCHE

• • •

Cease, every joy, to glimmer on my mind,
But leave—oh! leave the light of Hope behind.
—THOMAS CAMPBELL

• • •

You may say I'm a dreamer, but I'm not the only one.
I hope someday you'll join us.
And the world will live as one.
—JOHN LENNON

• • •

I believe that imagination is stronger than knowledge. That myth is more potent than history. That dreams are more powerful than facts. That hope always triumphs over experience. That laughter is the only cure for grief. And I believe that love is stronger than death.

—Robert Fulghum, *All I Really Need to Know I Learned in Kindergarten*

• • •

Yesterday is but a dream,
Tomorrow is only a vision.
But today well lived makes every yesterday a dream of happiness, and every tomorrow a vision of hope.
Look well, therefore, to this day. Such is the salutation to the dawn.

—Kālidāsa, *The Complete Works of Kālidāsa*

• • •

Do not follow me! Let's just be fabulously where we are and who we are. You be you and I'll be me, today and today and today, and let's trust the future to tomorrow. Let the stars keep track of us. Let us ride our own orbits and trust that they will meet. May our reunion be not a finding but a sweet collision of destinies!
—JERRY SPINELLI, *LOVE, STARGIRL*

• • •

Plant seeds of happiness, hope, success, and love; it will all come back to you in abundance. This is the law of nature.
—STEVE MARABOLI, *LIFE, THE TRUTH, AND BEING FREE*

• • •

There's a taste in the air, sweet and vaguely antiseptic, that reminds him of his teenage years in these streets, and of a general state of longing, a hunger for life to begin that from this distance seems like happiness.
—IAN MCEWAN, *SATURDAY*

• • •

I can hardly wait for tomorrow, it means a new life for me each and every day.
—STANLEY KUNITZ

• • •

But then, life is a constant withering of possibilities. Some are stolen with the lives of people you love. Others are let go, with regret and reluctance and deep, deep sorrow. But there is compensation for lives unlived in the intoxicating joy of knowing that the life you have—right here, right now—is the one you have chosen. There is power in that, and hope.

—EMILY MAGUIRE, *TAMING THE BEAST*

• • •

I'll make a swing so I can reach the places I can't reach yet.

—NINA LaCOUR, *HOLD STILL*

• • •

I have come to accept the feeling of not knowing where I am going. And I have trained myself to love it. Because it is only when we are suspended in mid-air with no landing in sight, that we force our wings to unravel and alas begin our flight. And as we fly, we still may not know where we are going to. But the miracle is in the unfolding of the wings. You may not know where you're going, but you know that so long as you spread your wings, the winds will carry you.

—C. JOYBELL C.

• • •

Every moment has its pleasures and its hope.
—Jane Austen, *Mansfield Park*

• • •

Happiness is as a butterfly which, when pursued, is always beyond our grasp, but which if you will sit down quietly, may alight upon you.
—Nathaniel Hawthorne

• • •

He'd do what he always did, find the sweet among the bitter.
—Jamie Ford, *Hotel on the Corner of Bitter and Sweet*

• • •

That was how it always was with Colleen: No matter how sad she felt, there was always this little bit of hope—like a speck of glitter caught in your eyelash—that never went away, no matter what.
—Lauren Tarshis, *Emma-Jean Lazarus Fell in Love*

• • •

Is it folly to believe in something that is intangible? After all, some of the greatest intangibles are Love, Hope, and Wonder.
—Vera Nazarian, *The Perpetual Calendar of Inspiration*

• • •

Be Cool, Stay Cool. Crazy Times in this Crazy World. Laugh your ass off, or die crying. To be alive, or to die. LIFE; Live it, Learn it, Love it, Become it.
—Laura E. Brusseau

• • •

What I need to survive is not Gale's fire, kindled with rage and hatred. I have plenty of fire myself. What I need is the dandelion in the spring. The bright yellow that means rebirth instead of destruction. The promise that life can go on, no matter how bad our losses.
—Suzanne Collins, *Mockingjay*

• • •

Regardless of how black the page, he had always managed to turn it and move on to a new chapter in his life.
—Robert Masello, *Blood and Ice*

• • •

A man is a fool to live in hopes of a better tomorrow. I have a thousand, better ways today to spend what time remains ahead of me, and I have brighter, lighter and more pleasant places in which to spend it.
—Jack Whyte, *Uther*

• • •

Spring is when you feel like whistling even with a shoe full of slush.
—Doug Larson

• • •

Being a cheerful hobbit, he had not needed hope, as long as despair could be postponed.
—J. R. R. Tolkien, *The Two Towers*

• • •

If you do follow your bliss you put yourself on a kind of track that has been there all the while, waiting for you, and the life that you ought to be living is the one you are living. When you can see that, you begin to meet people who are in your field of bliss, and they open doors to you. I say, follow your bliss and don't be afraid, and doors will open where you didn't know they were going to be.
—Joseph Campbell, *The Power of Myth*

• • •

But it is a blessed provision of nature that at times like these, as soon as a man's mercury has got down to a certain point there comes a revulsion, and he rallies. Hope springs up, and cheerfulness along with it, and then he is in good shape to do something for himself, if anything can be done.

—MARK TWAIN, *A CONNECTICUT YANKEE IN KING ARTHUR'S COURT*

• • •

We feasted, we laughed, we played games, lost and won, we told the best stories. And each week we could hope to be lucky. That hope was our only joy. And that's how we came to call our little parties Joy Luck.

—AMY TAN, *THE JOY LUCK CLUB*

• • •

There are some moments I feel those shards of my broken heart start to fit together. . . THAT is when I can actually celebrate. In that moment I find hope. . . I think it's in that moment that the world changes.

—MARILYN DE GUEHERY

• • •

There is neither happiness nor unhappiness in this world; there is only the comparison of one state with another. Only a man who has felt ultimate despair is capable of feeling ultimate bliss. It is necessary to have wished for death in order to know how good it is to live.
—ALEXANDRE DUMAS, *THE COUNT OF MONTE CRISTO*

• • •

I do not know what is happening. The reason of my waking mind tells me that great evil has befallen and we stand at the end of days. But my heart says nay; and all my limbs are light, and a hope and joy are come to me that no reason can deny. . . I do not believe that darkness will endure!
—J. R. R. TOLKIEN, *THE RETURN OF THE KING*

• • •

The positive emotions that arise in . . . unpromising circumstances demonstrate that social ties and meaningful work are deeply desired, readily improvised, and intensely rewarding. The very structure of our economy and society prevents these goals from being achieved.
—REBECCA SOLNIT, *A PARADISE BUILT IN HELL*

• • •

Joy

But a sanguine temper, though forever expecting more good than occurs, does not always pay for its hopes by any proportionate depression. It soon flies over the present failure, and begins to hope again.
—JANE AUSTEN, *EMMA*

• • •

"Faith, hope, and love," says Charles G. Ames, "are purifiers of the blood."
—NIXON WATERMAN, *THE GIRL WANTED*

• • •

Know then, whatever cheerful and serene
Supports the mind, supports the body too:
Hence, the most vital movement mortals feel
Is hope, the balm and lifeblood of the soul.
—JOHN ARMSTRONG, *ART OF PRESERVING HEALTH*

• • •

The natural flights of the human mind are not from pleasure to pleasure but from hope to hope.
—SAMUEL JOHNSON

• • •

Hope is sweet-minded and sweet-eyed. It draws pictures; it weaves fancies; it fills the future with delight.
—HENRY WARD BEECHER

• • •

Smiles give others hope, joy, and strength.
—WALT WHITMAN

• • •

My great hope is to laugh as much as I cry.
—MAYA ANGELOU

• • •

He that lives in hope danceth without music.
—GEORGE HERBERT

• • •

4

Love

Hope is the most exciting thing in life and if you honestly believe that love is out there, it will come. And even if it doesn't come straight away there is still that chance all through your life that it will.
—Josh Hartnett

• • •

Hope is only the love of life.
—Henri-Frédéric Amiel

• • •

The world is indeed full of peril and in it there are many dark places. But still there is much that is fair. And though in all lands, love is now mingled with grief, it still grows, perhaps, the greater.
—J. R. R. Tolkien, *The Fellowship of the Ring*

• • •

Ah, love, let us be true
To one another! for the world, which seems
To lie before us like a land of dreams,
So various, so beautiful, so new,
Hath really neither joy, nor love, nor light,

Nor certitude, nor peace, nor help for pain;
And we are here as on a darkling plain
Swept with confused alarms of struggle and flight,
Where ignorant armies clash by night.
—Matthew Arnold, "Dover Beach"

• • •

How far would you go to keep the hope of love alive?
—Nicholas Sparks, *The Choice*

• • •

I don't know when we'll see each other again or what the world will be like when we do. We may both have seen many horrible things. But I will think of you every time I need to be reminded that there is beauty and goodness in the world.
—ARTHUR GOLDEN, *MEMOIRS OF A GEISHA*

• • •

Hope is not about proving anything. It's about choosing to believe this one thing, that love is bigger than any grim, bleak shit anyone can throw at us.
—ANNE LAMOTT, *PLAN B: FURTHER THOUGHTS ON FAITH*

• • •

Turn around and believe that the good news that we are loved is better than we ever dared hope, and that to believe in that good news, to live out of it and toward it, to be in love with that good news, is of all glad things in this world the gladdest thing of all.
Amen, and come Lord Jesus.
—FREDERICK BUECHNER

• • •

The only way of knowing a person is to love them without hope.
—WALTER BENJAMIN

• • •

Long distance is hard. You have to trust that as you each change on your own, your relationship will also change along with you. It takes hope, good humor, and idealism. It takes a massive dose of courage to protect the relationship at all odds. It is hard, but worth it. You'll both be stronger as a result.
—CRAIG M. MULLANEY, *THE UNFORGIVING MINUTE: A SOLDIER'S EDUCATION*

• • •

Hey you, don't tell me there's no hope at all.
Together we stand, divided we fall.
—PINK FLOYD, "HEY YOU," *THE WALL*

• • •

It's funny how, in this journey of life, even though we may begin at different times and places, our paths cross with others so that we may share our love, compassion, observations, and hope. This is a design of God that I appreciate and cherish.
—STEVE MARABOLI, *LIFE, THE TRUTH, AND BEING FREE*

• • •

Love without hope will not survive.
Love without faith changes nothing.
Love gives power to hope and faith.
—Toba Beta, *My Ancestor Was an Ancient Astronaut*

• • •

And isn't the whole world yours? For how often you set it on fire with your love and saw it blaze and burn up and secretly replaced it with another world while everyone slept. You felt in such complete harmony with God, when every morning you asked him for a new earth, so that all the ones he had made could have their turn. You thought it would be shabby to save them and repair them; you used them up and held out your hands, again and again, for more world. For your love was equal to everything.
—Rainer Maria Rilke, *The Notebooks of Malte Laurids Brigge*

• • •

But love, like the sun that it is, sets afire and melts everything.
What greed and privilege to build up over whole centuries
the indignation of a pious spirit, with its natural following of
oppressed souls, will cast down with a single shove.
—José Martí

• • •

Hope is the greatest madness. What can we expect of a world that
we enter with the assurance of seeing our fathers and mothers
die? A world where, if two beings love each other and give their
lives to each other, both can be sure that one will watch the other
perish?
—Alfred de Vigny, *Stello*

• • •

And I sometimes think that a moment of touching is the
difference between complete utter despair and
the ability to carry on.
—Eleanor Cameron, *The Court of the Stone Children*

• • •

Love

In some not too distant tomorrow the radiant stars of love and brotherhood will shine over our great nation with all their scintillating beauty.
—DR. MARTIN LUTHER KING JR., *THE AUTOBIOGRAPHY OF MARTIN LUTHER KING JR.*

• • •

I wanted to see the place where Margaret grew to what she is, even at the worst time of all, when I had no hope of ever calling her mine. . .
—ELIZABETH GASKELL, *NORTH AND SOUTH*

• • •

Home was not a perfect place. But it was the only home they had and they could hope to make it better.
—DEAN KOONTZ, *WINTER MOON*

• • •

Hope in the beginning feels like such a violation of the loss, and yet without it we couldn't survive.
—GAIL CALDWELL, *LET'S TAKE THE LONG WAY HOME: A MEMOIR OF FRIENDSHIP*

• • •

His hope wasn't lost, it was buried, and somehow Prudence Ryland made that old grave seem much more shallow than it once was.
—KATHRYN SMITH

• • •

Fair as the moon and joyful as the light;
Not wan with waiting, not with sorrow dim;
Not as she is, but was when hope shone bright;
Not as she is, but as she fills his dreams.
—CHRISTINA ROSSETTI

• • •

There is no hope for the hopeless but there is always some love for the loveless.
—SANTOSH KALWAR

• • •

Hope and faith underlie a promise, and love energizes men to realize it.
—TOBA BETA, *MY ANCESTOR WAS AN ANCIENT ASTRONAUT*

• • •

The key is love
It is the gateway
To hope
To joy
To enhanced living
Love is the answer.
—Karen Hackel, *The Whisper of Your Soul*

• • •

I have no word of yours to assure me that our brief friendship held for you the same significance it held for me, but I must go on believing so. Every hope of the future is meaningless unless I have faith that you and I will share it together.
—Elizabeth George Speare, *Calico Captive*

• • •

Dear refuge of my weary soul,
On thee, when sorrows rise,
On thee, when waves of trouble roll,
My fainting hope relies.
—ANNE STEELE

• • •

Love is a springtime plant that perfumes everything with its
hope, even the ruins to which it clings.
—GUSTAV FLAUBERT

• • •

All that I am or hope to be I owe to my angel mother.
— ABRAHAM LINCOLN

• • •

Love

A small degree of hope is enough to cause the birth of love.
—STENDHAL

• • •

Marriage is like putting your hand in a bag of snakes in the hope
of pulling out an eel.
—LEONARDO DA VINCI

• • •

We have to accept that the people we love do not love us, or not
in the way we hope.
—SÁNDOR MÁRAI

• • •

5

Despair

Abandon hope all ye who enter here.
—DANTE ALIGHIERI, *DANTE'S INFERNO*

• • •

He who despairs over an event is a coward, but he who holds
hope for the human condition is a fool.
—ALBERT CAMUS, *THE REBEL*

• • •

He that lives upon hope will die fasting.
—BENJAMIN FRANKLIN

• • •

He who has never hoped can never despair.
—GEORGE BERNARD SHAW, *CAESAR AND CLEOPATRA*

● ● ●

Take hope from the heart of man, and you make him a beast of prey.
—QUIDA

● ● ●

Appetite, with an opinion of attaining, is called hope; the same, without such opinion, despair.
—THOMAS HOBBES

● ● ●

I can endure my own despair,
but not another's hope.
—WILLIAM WALSH

● ● ●

Life is under no obligation to give us what we expect.
—MARGARET MITCHELL

● ● ●

The best way to not feel hopeless is to get up and do something.
Don't wait for good things to happen to you. If you go out and
make some good things happen, you will fill the world with hope,
you will fill yourself with hope.
—Barack Obama

• • •

There is a saying in Tibetan, "Tragedy should be utilized as a
source of strength."
No matter what sort of difficulties, how painful experience is, if
we lose our hope, that's our real disaster.
—Dalai Lama XIV

• • •

To hear the phrase "our only hope" always makes one anxious,
because it means that if the only hope doesn't work, there is
nothing left.
—Lemony Snicket, The Blank Book

• • •

Oft hope is born when all is forlorn.
—J. R. R. Tolkien, The Return of the King

• • •

If we will be quiet and ready enough, we shall find compensation
in every disappointment.
—HENRY DAVID THOREAU

• • •

"What hope is there?" I asked. "If even angels fall, what hope is
there for the rest of us?"
—RICHELLE MEAD, SUCCUBUS DREAMS

• • •

Where there is no hope, it is incumbent on us to invent it.
—ALBERT CAMUS

• • •

The heart dies, a slow death,
shedding each hope like leaves . . .
. . . until one day there are
none. No hopes. Nothing remains.
—ARTHUR GOLDEN, MEMOIRS OF A GEISHA

• • •

You might think I lost all hope at that point. I did. And as a result
I perked up and felt much better.
—YANN MARTEL, *LIFE OF PI*

• • •

Deep grief sometimes is almost like a specific location, a
coordinate on a map of time. When you are standing in that
forest of sorrow, you cannot imagine that you could ever find
your way to a better place. But if someone can assure you that
they themselves have stood in that same place, and now have
moved on, sometimes this will bring hope.
—ELIZABETH GILBERT, *EAT, PRAY, LOVE*

• • •

I want to believe that I'm not wrong. I want to believe that life
isn't full of darkness. Even if storms come to pass, the sun will
shine again. No matter how painful and hard the rain may beat
down on me.
—NATSUKI TAKAYA

• • •

She wondered that hope was so much harder than despair.
—PATRICIA BRIGGS, *CRY WOLF*

• • •

Those who make us believe that anything's possible and fire our imagination over the long haul, are often the ones who have survived the bleakest of circumstances. The men and women who have every reason to despair, but don't, may have the most to teach us, not only about how to hold true to our beliefs, but about how such a life can bring about seemingly impossible social change.
—PAUL ROGAT LOEB, *THE IMPOSSIBLE WILL TAKE A LITTLE WHILE: A CITIZEN'S GUIDE TO HOPE IN A TIME OF FEAR*

• • •

Remind thyself, in the darkest moments, that every failure is only a step toward success, every detection of what is false directs you toward what is true, every trial exhausts some tempting form of error, and every adversity will only hide, for a time, your path to peace and fulfillment.
—OG MANDINO

• • •

I laugh because I must not cry, that is all, that is all.
—ABRAHAM LINCOLN

• • •

When you're at the end of your rope, tie a knot and hold on.
—THEODORE ROOSEVELT

• • •

People have hope because they cannot see Death standing behind
them.
—TITE KUBO

• • •

But all I could think of was how when nothing made sense and
hadn't for ages, you just have to grab onto anything you feel
sure of.
—SARAH DESSEN, *THE TRUTH ABOUT FOREVER*

• • •

Hope is such a beautiful word, but it often seems very fragile. Life is still being needlessly hurt and destroyed.
—MICHAEL JACKSON

• • •

That was all a man needed: hope. It was lack of hope that discouraged a man.
—CHARLES BUKOWSKI, *FACTOTUM*

• • •

There was a moment in my life when I really wanted to kill myself. And there was one other moment when I was close to that . . . But even in my most jaded times, I had some hope.
—GERARD WAY

• • •

Hope is the last thing a person does before they are defeated.
—HENRY ROLLINS

• • •

Despair

There is a secret medicine given only to those who hurt so hard
they can't hope.
The hopers would feel slighted if they knew.
—RUMI, *THE ESSENTIAL RUMI*

● ● ●

Despair is typical of those who do not understand the causes of
evil, see no way out, and are incapable of struggle.
—VLADIMIR ILYICH LENIN

● ● ●

The Fourteenth Book is entitled, "What can a Thoughtful Man
Hope for Mankind on Earth, Given the Experience of the Past
Million Years?"
It doesn't take long to read The Fourteenth Book. It consists of
one word and a period.
This is it: "Nothing."
—KURT VONNEGUT, *CAT'S CRADLE*

● ● ●

Sir Topher finally looked up. "Because any hope beyond that, my boy, would be too much. I feared we would drown in it."
"Then I choose to drown," Finnikin said. "In hope. Rather than float into nothing."
—MELINA MARCHETTA, *FINNIKIN OF THE ROCK*

• • •

There had to be dark and muddy waters so that the sun could have something to background its flashing glory.
—BETTY SMITH

• • •

"Look," he said, "the point is there's no way to be a hundred percent sure about anyone or anything. So you're left with a choice. Either hope for the best, or just expect the worst."
"If you expect the worst, you're never disappointed," I pointed out.
"Yeah, but who lives like that?"
—SARAH DESSEN, *LOCK AND KEY*

• • •

A great Hope fell
You heard no noise
The Ruin was within.
—EMILY DICKINSON

• • •

We need never be hopeless because we can never be irreparably
broken.
—JOHN GREEN, *LOOKING FOR ALASKA*

• • •

We look into each other's eyes as we shake. His are still full of
death and horror, but in them I see my face reflected, and inside
my tiny eyes inside his, I think I see some hope.
—NED VIZZINI, *IT'S KIND OF A FUNNY STORY*

• • •

But what is Hope? Nothing but the paint on the face of Existence; the least touch of truth rubs it off, and then we see what a hollow-cheeked harlot we have got hold of.
—LORD BYRON

• • •

To hope for nothing, to expect nothing, to demand nothing. This is analytical despair.
—JAMES HILLMAN, *SUICIDE AND THE SOUL*

• • •

I came to the conclusion that unrealized hopes, even small ones, were always wrenching.
—NICHOLAS SPARKS, *THE WEDDING*

• • •

Man can live about forty days without food, about three days without water, about eight minutes without air . . . but only for one second without hope.
—HAL LINDSEY

• • •

The road that is built in hope is more pleasant to the traveler than the road built in despair, even though they both lead to the same destination.
—MARION ZIMMER BRADLEY, *THE FALL OF ATLANTIS*

• • •

A loss of any kind is horrible. Not because it takes away, but because it makes you believe—in newspapers, in tomatoes, in empty whiskey bottles.
—ANOSH IRANI, *THE CRIPPLE AND HIS TALISMANS*

• • •

The only hope for the doomed, is no hope at all. . .
—VIRGIL, *THE AENEID*

• • •

I think hope is the worst thing in the world. I really do. It makes a fool of you while it lasts. And then when it's gone, it's like there's nothing left of you at all . . . except what you can't be rid of.
—MARILYNNE ROBINSON, *HOME*

• • •

Hope was an instinct only the reasoning human mind could kill.
An animal never knew despair.
—GRAHAM GREENE, *THE POWER AND THE GLORY*

• • •

To be truly radical is to make hope possible rather than despair
convincing.
—RAYMOND WILLIAMS

• • •

. . . a cynic who was still saddened whenever his jaundiced view
of mankind was confirmed. . .
—SHARON KAY PENMAN, *WHEN CHRIST AND HIS SAINTS
SLEPT*

• • •

It's true I live on hope. Why shouldn't I? Every day I see her
beauty while you rot in hell. You will tell me that I'm deluded but
we are all deluded in some way. The question is which is the best
delusion.
—DANNY SCHEINMANN, *RANDOM ACTS OF HEROIC LOVE*

• • •

Despair

Faith seems to grab people and not let go, but hope is a double-crosser. It can beat it on you anytime; it's your job to dig in your heels and hang on. Must be nice to have hope in your pocket, like loose change you could jingle through your fingers.
—Judy Blundell, *Strings Attached*

• • •

Do try to remember this: even the world's not so black as it is painted.
—Radclyffe Hall, *The Well of Loneliness*

• • •

"Hope?" he says. "There is always hope, John. New developments have yet to present themselves. Not all the information is in. No. Don't give up hope just yet. It's the last thing to go. When you have lost hope, you have lost everything. And when you think all is lost, when all is dire and bleak, there is always hope."
—Pittacus Lore, *I Am Number Four*

• • •

By the time the last few notes fade, his hope will be restored, but each time he's forced to resort to the Adagio it becomes harder, and he knows its effect is finite. There are only a certain number of Adagios left in him, and he will not recklessly spend this precious currency.
—STEVEN GALLOWAY

• • •

What disturbs and depresses young people is the hunt for happiness on the firm assumption that it must be met with in life. From this arises constantly deluded hope and so also dissatisfaction. Deceptive images of a vague happiness hover before us in our dreams, and we search in vain for their original. Much would have been gained if, through timely advice and instruction, young people could have had eradicated from their minds the erroneous notion that the world has a great deal to offer them.
—ARTHUR SCHOPENHAUER

• • •

How fortunate we were who still had hope I did not then realise; I could not know how soon the time would come when we should have no more hope, and yet be unable to die.
—VERA BRITTAIN, *TESTAMENT OF YOUTH*

• • •

Always try to find hope in the worst situations, and that will make all the difference.
—Taylor Mitchum

• • •

David's mouth dripped open slowly. He stood with his heels dug into my carpet, a dashed hope, a broken dream. No amount of money could top the priceless look that gathered on his face like an unmade bed. His eyebrows crumpled and furrowed like disheveled sheets. His lips curled into an acidic smirk. Confusion and shock collided in the cornea of his dilated pupils. He was a B.B. King song, personified. His entire body sang the blues.
—Brandi L. Bates, *Quirk*

• • •

A man devoid of hope and conscious of being so has ceased to belong to the future.
—Albert Camus, *The Myth of Sisyphus and Other Essays*

• • •

But, oh, when gloomy doubts prevail,
I fear to call thee mine;
The springs of comfort seem to fail,
And all my hopes decline.
—Anne Steele

• • •

"Oh no," I said, because if our life is just one endless song about
hope and regret, then "oh no" is apparently that song's chorus, the
words we always return to.
—Brock Clarke, *An Arsonist's Guide to Writers'
Homes in New England*

• • •

Don't hope you will receive help from the words of life because
they all bring you to death.
—Sorin Cerin, *Wisdom Collection*

• • •

Not, I'll not, carrion comfort, Despair, not feast on thee;
Not untwist—slack they may be—these last strands of man
In me or, most weary, cry I can no more. I can;
Can something, hope, wish day come, not choose not to be.
—Gerard Manley Hopkins

• • •

Despair is for people who know, beyond any doubt, what the future is going to bring. Nobody is in that position. So despair is not only a kind of sin, theologically, but also a simple mistake, because nobody actually knows. In that sense there is always hope.
—PATRICK CURRY, *DEFENDING MIDDLE-EARTH: TOLKIEN: MYTH AND MODERNITY*

• • •

The heart bowed down by weight of woe
To weakest hope will cling.
—ALFRED BUNN, *THE BOHEMIAN GIRL*

• • •

We always hope, and in all things it is better to hope than to despair.
—JOHANN WOLFGANG VON GOETHE, *TORQUATO TASSO*

• • •

Let no one despair, even though in the darkest night the last star of hope may disappear.
—FRIEDRICH SCHILLER, *OBERON*

• • •

Hope is the worst of all evils because it prolongs the torments of man.
—Friedrich Nietzsche

• • •

. . . what we call our despair is often only the painful eagerness of unfed hope.
—George Eliot

• • •

Hope is a horrible thing, you know. I don't know who decided to package hope as a virtue, because it's not. It's a plague. Hope is like walking around with a fishhook in your mouth and somebody just keeps pulling it and pulling it.
—Ann Patchett, *State of Wonder*

• • •

Despair

Hope, whose whisper would have given
Balm to all my frenzied pain,
Stretched her wings, and soared to heaven,
Went, and ne'er returned again.
—EMILY BRONTË

● ● ●

He that lives upon hope will die fasting.
—BENJAMIN FRANKLIN

● ● ●

There is an infinite amount of hope in the universe . . . but not for
us.
—FRANZ KAFKA

● ● ●

If you lose all hope you can always find it again.
—RICHARD FORD

● ● ●

6

Inspiration

Learn from yesterday, live for today, hope for tomorrow. The important thing is not to stop questioning.
—ALBERT EINSTEIN

• • •

There is hope in dreams, imagination, and in the courage of those who wish to make those dreams a reality.
—JONAS SALK

• • •

To do something, however small, to make others happier and better, is the highest ambition, the most elevating hope, which can inspire a human being.
—John Lubbock

• • •

To love means loving the unlovable. To forgive means pardoning the unpardonable. Faith means believing the unbelievable. Hope means hoping when everything seems hopeless.
—G. K. Chesterton

• • •

Until the day when God shall deign to reveal the future to man, all human wisdom is summed up in these two words,—"Wait and hope."
—Alexandre Dumas, *The Count of Monte Cristo*

• • •

Do not spoil what you have by desiring what you have not; but remember that what you now have was once among the things you only hoped for.
—Epicurus

• • •

Hope, like the gleaming taper's light,
Adorns and cheers our way;
And still, as darker grows the night,
Emits a brighter ray.
—Oliver Goldsmith

• • •

It is difficult to say what is impossible, for the dream of yesterday is the hope of today and the reality of tomorrow.
—Robert H. Goddard

• • •

It's really a wonder that I haven't dropped all my ideals, because they seem so absurd and impossible to carry out. Yet I keep them, because in spite of everything I still believe that people are really good at heart.
—ANNE FRANK, *THE DIARY OF A YOUNG GIRL*

• • •

It is often in the darkest
skies that we see the
brightest stars.
—RICHARD EVANS

• • •

For like a shaft, clear and cold, the thought pierced him that in the end the Shadow was only a small and passing thing: there was light and high beauty for ever beyond its reach.
—J. R. R. TOLKIEN, *THE RETURN OF THE KING*

• • •

Walk on with hope in your heart,
and you'll never walk alone
—SHAHRUKH KHAN

• • •

It isn't as bad as you sometimes think it is. It all works out. Don't worry. I say that to myself every morning. It all works out in the end. Put your trust in God, and move forward with faith and confidence in the future. The Lord will not forsake us. He will not forsake us. If we will put our trust in Him, if we will pray to Him, if we will live worthy of His blessings, He will hear our prayers.
—GORDON B. HINCKLEY

• • •

All of a sudden, this shooting star went by, and all I could think was that they were listening to us somehow.
—NICHOLAS SPARKS, *THE LUCKY ONE*

• • •

Remember, Hope is a good thing, maybe the best of things, and no good thing ever dies.
—STEPHEN KING, *THE SHAWSHANK REDEMPTION*

• • •

I am fundamentally an optimist. Whether that comes from nature or nurture, I cannot say. Part of being optimistic is keeping one's head pointed toward the sun, one's feet moving forward. There were many dark moments when my faith in humanity was sorely tested, but I would not and could not give myself up to despair. That way lies defeat and death.
—NELSON MANDELA, *LONG WALK TO FREEDOM: AUTOBIOGRAPHY OF NELSON MANDELA*

• • •

Now, faith is being sure of what we hope for and certain of what we do not see.
—*HOLY BIBLE: NEW INTERNATIONAL VERSION*

• • •

God is always there for you even when someone is gone. He helps you cope with things that make you hurt, and leads you by the hand to happiness again.
—MISS READ

• • •

We're called to be faithful, to take those first difficult steps—and to leave the results up to God.
—ALEX HARRIS

• • •

Do not lose hope—what you seek will be found. Trust ghosts. Trust those that you have helped to help you in their turn. Trust dreams. Trust your heart, and trust your story.
—Neil Gaiman, *Fragile Things*

• • •

I inhale hope with every breath I take.
—Sharon Kay Penman, *When Christ and His Saints Slept*

• • •

Faith goes up the stairs that love has built and looks out the windows which hope has opened.
—Charles H. Spurgeon

• • •

Ad astra per aspera. (To the stars through difficulties.)
—Seneca

• • •

Faith is the very first thing you should pack in a hope chest.
—Sarah Ban Breathnach

• • •

Keep your best wishes close to your heart and watch
what happens.
—Tony Deliso, *Legacy: The Power Within*

• • •

We should ask God to increase our hope when it is small, awaken
it when it is dormant, confirm it when it is wavering, strengthen
it when it is weak, and raise it up when it is overthrown.
—John Calvin

• • •

Therefore, since we are receiving a kingdom that cannot be
shaken, let us be thankful, and so worship God acceptably with
reverence and awe, for our God is a consuming fire.
—Hebrews 12:28–29

• • •

Perhaps it takes a purer faith to praise God for unrealized blessings than for those we once enjoyed or those we enjoy now.
—A. W. Tozer

• • •

To have Christian hope means to know about evil and yet to go to meet the future with confidence. The core of faith rests upon accepting being loved by God, and therefore to believe is to say Yes, not only to him, but to creation, to creatures, above all, to men, to try to see the image of God in each person and thereby to become a lover. That's not easy, but the basic Yes, the conviction that God has created men, that he stands behind them, that they aren't simply negative, gives love a reference point that enables it to ground hope on the basis of faith.
—Pope Benedict XVI

• • •

If you follow the will of God, you know that in spite of all the terrible things that happen to you, you will never lose a final refuge. You know that the foundation of the world is love, so that even when no human being can or will help you, you may go on, trusting in the One that loves you.
—Pope Benedict XVI

• • •

We're here for a reason. I believe a bit of the reason is to throw little torches out to lead people through the dark.
—WHOOPI GOLDBERG

• • •

I feel no need for any other faith than my faith in the kindness of human beings. I am so absorbed in the wonder of earth and the life upon it that I cannot think of heaven and angels.
—PEARL S. BUCK, *I BELIEVE*

• • •

Passion means suffering and compassion means suffering together. Suffering produces perseverance and perseverance produces character and character produces hope. And that lifts people up, knowing they're not alone.
—LACEY MOSLEY

• • •

To hope under the most extreme circumstances is an act of defiance that permits a person to live his life on his own terms. It is part of the human spirit to endure and give a miracle a chance to happen.
—JEROME GROOPMAN

• • •

So when you feel like hope is gone
Look inside you and be strong
And you'll finally see the truth
That a hero lies in you.
—MARIAH CAREY

• • •

There is hope in forgiveness.
—JOHN PIPER, *A SWEET AND BITTER PROVIDENCE: SEX,
RACE, AND THE SOVEREIGNTY OF GOD*

• • •

Once you choose hope, anything's possible.
—CHRISTOPHER REEVE

• • •

To have faith is to be sure of the things we hope for, to be certain
of the things we cannot see.
—*HEBREWS 11:1*

• • •

Let my body dwell in poverty, and my hands be as the hands of the toiler; but let my soul be as a temple of remembrance where the treasures of knowledge enter and the inner sanctuary is hope.
—GEORGE ELIOT, *DANIEL DERONDA*

• • •

Broken heart will turn into a stronger one within hope.
—TOBA BETA, *MY ANCESTOR WAS AN ANCIENT ASTRONAUT*

• • •

Sometimes when you least expect it, the tables turn and that scary feeling that has taken hold of you for so long somehow turns into hope.
—DAVID ARCHULETA, *CHORDS OF STRENGTH: A MEMOIR OF SOUL, SONG, AND THE POWER OF PERSEVERANCE*

• • •

And as I watched him, I knew that in every dark night there was, somewhere, a small light burning that could never be quenched.
—JULIET MARILLIER, *SON OF THE SHADOWS*

• • •

We shall find peace. We shall hear the angels, we shall see the sky sparkling with diamonds.
—ANTON CHEKHOV, *UNCLE VANYA*

• • •

Life without thankfulness is devoid of love and passion. Hope without thankfulness is lacking in fine perception. Faith without thankfulness lacks strength and fortitude. Every virtue divorced from thankfulness is maimed and limps along the spiritual road.
—JOHN HENRY JOWETT

• • •

The greatest act of faith some days is to simply get up and face
another day.
—AMY GATLIFF

• • •

Euripedes. Nothing is hopeless; we must hope for everything.
—MADELEINE L'ENGLE, *A WRINKLE IN TIME*

• • •

Faith, hope, and charity go together. Hope is practised through
the virtue of patience, which continues to do good even in the
face of apparent failure, and through the virtue of humility, which
accepts God's mystery and trusts him even at times of darkness.
—POPE BENEDICT XVI

• • •

What we have at the moment isn't as the old liturgies used to say,
"the sure and certain hope of the resurrection of the dead," but a
vague and fuzzy optimism that somehow things may work out in
the end.
—N. T. WRIGHT, *SURPRISED BY HOPE*

• • •

Great hope has no real footing unless one is willing to face into the doom that may also be on the way.
—NORMAN MAILER AND JOHN BUFFALO MAILER, *THE BIG EMPTY: DIALOGUES ON POLITICS, SEX, GOD, BOXING, MORALITY, MYTH, POKER & BAD CONSCIENCE IN AMERICA*

• • •

Sometimes that
which we fear
strengthens our
spirit and gives
us a splash
of hope.
—HARLEY KING

• • •

Hope and faith go hand-in-hand, because without hope there is no faith. The same goes with want and needs, without any wants, there no need to have a need.
—TEMITOPE OWOSELA

• • •

Inspiration

Hope is something that is demanded of us; it is not, then, a mere reasoned calculation of our chances. Nor is it merely the bubbling up of a sanguine temperament; if it is demanded of us, it lies not in the temperament but in the will. . . Hoping for what? For deliverance from persecution, for immunity from plague, pestilence, and famine . . . ? No, for the grace of persevering in his Christian profession, and for the consequent achievement of a happy immortality. Strictly speaking, then, the highest exercise of hope, supernaturally speaking, is to hope for perseverance and for Heaven when it looks, when it feels, as if you were going to lose both one and the other.

—RONALD A. KNOX

• • •

Fiction cannot recite the numbing numbers, but it can be that witness, that memory. A storyteller can attempt to tell the human tale, can make a galaxy out of the chaos, can point to the fact that some people survived even as most people died. And can remind us that the swallows still sing around the smokestacks.

—JANE YOLEN

• • •

God grant me the courage not to give up what I think is right,
even though I think it is hopeless.
—CHESTER NIMITZ

• • •

Hope is some extraordinary spiritual grace that God gives us to
control our fears, not to oust them.
—VINCENT JOSEPH MCNABB

• • •

If justice takes place, there may be hope, even in the face of a
seemingly capricious divinity.
—ALBERTO MANGUEL, *THE LIBRARY AT NIGHT*

• • •

Hope has two beautiful daughters: their names are anger and
courage. Anger that things are the way they are. Courage to make
them the way they ought to be.
—AUGUSTINE OF HIPPO

• • •

If you have abandoned one faith, do not abandon all faith. There is always an alternative to the faith we lose. Or is it the same faith under another name?
—GRAHAM GREENE

• • •

At present we are on the outside of the world, the wrong side of the door. We discern the freshness and purity of the morning, but they do not make us fresh and pure. We cannot mingle with the splendours we see. But all the leaves of the New Testament are rustling with the rumour that it will not always be so. Some day, God willing, we shall get in.
—C. S. LEWIS, *THE WEIGHT OF GLORY*

• • •

God can inject hope into an absolutely hopeless situation.
—MARK EVANS

• • •

If there's only one nation in the sky, shouldn't all passports be valid for it?
—YANN MARTEL, *LIFE OF PI*

• • •

Christian hope frees us to act hopefully in the world. It enables us to act humbly and patiently, tackling visible injustices in the world around us without needing to be assured that our skill and our effort will somehow rid the world of injustice altogether. Christian hope, after all, does not need to see what it hopes for [Heb. 11:1].
—CRAIG M. GAY, *THE WAY OF THE (MODERN) WORLD*

• • •

There's no guarantee of disaster-free in any world religion, but love, faith and knowledge give men hope and willpower.
—TOBA BETA, *MY ANCESTOR WAS AN ANCIENT ASTRONAUT*

• • •

Unfortunates, who ought to begin with God, do not have any hope in him till they have exhausted all other means of deliverance.
—ALEXANDRE DUMAS, *THE COUNT OF MONTE CRISTO*

• • •

But we believe—nay, Lord we only hope,
That one day we shall thank thee perfectly
For pain and hope and all that led or drove
Us back into the bosom of thy love.
—GEORGE MACDONALD

• • •

Dullness it is that perverts and corrupts the spirit but it is always possible to look past the dullness, and see the bright, shining heart of things.
—JUDE MORGAN, *INDISCRETION*

• • •

Lord save us all from . . . a hope tree that has lost the faculty of putting out blossoms.
—MARK TWAIN

• • •

Exactly at the instant when hope ceases to be reasonable, it begins to be useful.
—G. K. CHESTERTON

• • •

Extreme hopes are born of extreme misery.
—BERTRAND RUSSELL

• • •

If you do not hope, you will not find what is beyond your hopes.
—CLEMENT OF ALEXANDRIA

• • •

. . . to hope till Hope creates
From its own wreck the thing it contemplates.
—Percy Bysshe Shelley

• • •

The fact that there is only a spiritual world robs us of hope and
gives us certainty.
—Franz Kafka

• • •

There is hope in dreams, imagination, and in the courage of those
who wish to make those dreams a reality.
—Jonas Salk

• • •

To live without hope is to cease to live.
—Fyodor Dostoyevsky

• • •

7

Aspiration

All the great things are simple, and many can be expressed in a single word: Freedom; justice; honor; duty; mercy; hope.
—Winston Churchill

• • •

Most of the important things in the world have been accomplished by people who have kept on trying when there seemed to be no hope at all.
—Dale Carnegie

• • •

I know how men in exile feed on dreams of hope.
—Aeschylus, *Agamemnon*

• • •

Hope doesn't come from calculating whether the good news is winning out over the bad. It's simply a choice to take action.
—ANNA LAPPE, *O, THE OPRAH MAGAZINE*, JUNE 2003

• • •

Hope begins in the dark, the stubborn hope that if you just show up and try to do the right thing, the dawn will come. You wait and watch and work: You don't give up.
—ANNE LAMOTT

• • •

We have been told we cannot do this by a chorus of cynics. They will only grow louder and more dissonant in the weeks to come. We've been asked to pause for a reality check; we've been warned against offering the people of this nation false hope. But in the unlikely story that is America, there has never been anything false about hope.
—BARACK OBAMA

• • •

True hope is swift, and flies with swallow's wings;
Kings it makes gods, and meaner creatures kings.
—WILLIAM SHAKESPEARE, *KING RICHARD III*

• • •

When we love, we always strive to become better than we are.
When we strive to become better than we are, everything around
us becomes better too.
—Paulo Coelho, *The Alchemist*

• • •

One lives in the hope of becoming a memory.
—Antonio Porchia

• • •

In a time of destruction, create something.
—Maxine Hong Kingston

• • •

Everyone must dream. We dream to give ourselves hope. To stop
dreaming—well, that's like saying you can never change your fate.
Isn't that true?
—Amy Tan, *The Hundred Secret Senses*

• • •

In a world filled with hate, we must still dare to hope. In a world filled with anger, we must still dare to comfort. In a world filled with despair, we must still dare to dream. And in a world filled with distrust, we must still dare to believe.
—MICHAEL JACKSON

• • •

One resolution I have made, and try always to keep, is this: "To rise above little things."
—JOHN BURROUGHS

• • •

If you lose hope, somehow you lose the vitality that keeps moving, you lose that courage to be, that quality that helps you go on in spite of it all. And so today I still have a dream.
—DR. MARTIN LUTHER KING JR.

• • •

My hope still is to leave the world a bit better than when I got here.
—JIM HENSON

• • •

Aspiration

The miracle of man is not how far he has sunk but how
magnificently he has risen. We are known among the stars by our
poems, not our corpses.
—ROBERT ARDREY

• • •

I spit on your happiness! I spit on your idea of life—that life
that must go on, come what may. You are all like dogs that lick
everything they smell. You with your promise of a humdrum
happiness—provided a person doesn't ask much of life. I
want everything of life, I do; and I want it now! I want it total,
complete: otherwise I reject it! I will not be moderate. I will not
be satisfied with the bit of cake you offer me if I promise to be a
good little girl. I want to be sure of everything this very day; sure
that everything will be as beautiful as when I was a little girl. If
not, I want to die!
—JEAN ANOUILH, *ANTIGONE*

• • •

There is nothing more majestic than the determined courage of individuals willing to suffer and sacrifice for their freedom and dignity.
—DR. MARTIN LUTHER KING JR., *THE AUTOBIOGRAPHY OF MARTIN LUTHER KING JR.*

• • •

When you have a great and difficult task, something perhaps almost impossible, if you only work a little at a time, every day a little, suddenly the work will finish itself.
—KAREN BLIXEN

• • •

The times are chaotic. For me, I would hope that people look at [*Angel*] and gain strength by it. With everything that I do, I hope that they see people struggling to live decent, moral lives in a completely chaotic world. They see how hard it is, how often they fail, and how they get up and keep trying. That, to me, is the most important message I'm ever going to tell.
—JOSS WHEDON

• • •

We know the battle ahead will be long, but always remember that no matter what obstacles stand in our way, nothing can stand in the way of the power of millions of voices calling for change.
—BARACK OBAMA

• • •

"It all counts," Adam said again. "And the bottom line is, what defines you isn't how many times you crash, but the number of times you get back on the bike. As long as it's one more, you're all good."
—SARAH DESSEN, *ALONG FOR THE RIDE*

• • •

A person can do incredible things if he or she has enough hope.
—SHANNON K. BUTCHER

• • •

Men and women are not limited by the place of their birth, not by color of their skin, but by the size of their hope.
—JOHN JOHNSON

• • •

What makes a hero? Courage, strength, morality, withstanding adversity? Are these the traits that truly show and create a hero? Is the light truly the source of darkness or vice versa? Is the soul a source of hope or despair?
—FYODOR DOSTOYEVSKY, *NOTES FROM UNDERGROUND*

• • •

The restless spirit never loses its wings. If sometimes it cannot fly,
it is because during those moments the sky vanishes.
—R. N. Prasher

• • •

When today fails to offer the justification for hope, tomorrow
becomes the only grail worth pursuing.
—Christopher Bigsby

• • •

We are alive. We are human, with good and bad in us. That's all
we know for sure. We can't create a new species or a new world.
That's been done. Now we have to live within those boundaries.
What are our choices? We can despair and curse, and change
nothing. We can choose evil like our enemies have done and
create a world based on hate. Or we can try to make things better.
—Carol Matas, *Daniel's Story*

• • •

One often has to do what they have to do in order to do what they want to do; however if you only do what you want to do then you will never do what you have to do!
—DR. C. MOORER, *FROM FAILURE TO PROMISE: AN UNCOMMON PATH TO PROFESSORIATE*

• • •

So this is my cue of where to leave you. Now it's your story to retell and pass on. Because an idea is only relevant if it's being thought upon. So remember, never surrender. 'Cause the unrelenting constancy of love and hope will rescue and restore from any scope.
—THOMAS DUTTON

• • •

Remain faithful to the earth, my brothers, with the power of your virtue. Let your gift-giving love and your knowledge serve the meaning of the earth. Thus I beg and beseech you. Do not let them fly away from earthly things and beat with their wings against eternal walls. Alas, there has always been so much virtue that has flown away. Lead back to the earth the virtue that flew away, as I do—back to the body, back to life, that it may give the earth a meaning, a human meaning.
—FRIEDRICH NIETZSCHE

• • •

The mystic chords of memory, stretching from every battle-field and patriot grave, to every living heart and hearth-stone, all over this broad land, will yet swell the chorus of the Union, when again touched, as surely they will be, by the better angels of our nature.
—ABRAHAM LINCOLN

• • •

There is hope in dreams, imagination, and in the courage of those who wish to make those dreams a reality.
—JONAS SALK

• • •

. . . I believe in hope, in what is something called "radical hope." I believe there is hope for all of us, even amid the suffering. And that's why I write fiction, probably. It's my attempt to keep that fragile strand of radical hope, to build a fire in the darkness.
—JOHN GREEN

• • •

I believe that we are lost here in America, but I believe we shall be found. And this belief, which mounts now to the catharsis of knowledge and conviction, is for me—and I think for all of us—not only our own hope, but America's everlasting, living dream.
—THOMAS WOLFE

• • •

Wherever the hope of glory lives, hopelessness passes away.
—NADINE C. KEELS, *THE SONG OF NADINE*

• • •

In these downbeat times, we need as much hope and courage as we do vision and analysis; we must accent the best of each other even as we point out the vicious effects of our racial divide and pernicious consequences of our maldistribution of wealth and power.
—CORNEL WEST, *RACE MATTERS*

• • •

Hope is not blind optimism. It's not ignoring the enormity of the task ahead or the roadblocks that stand in our path. It's not sitting on the sidelines or shirking from a fight. Hope is that thing inside us that insists, despite all evidence to the contrary, that something better awaits us if we have the courage to reach for it, and to work for it, and to fight for it. Hope is the belief that destiny will not be written for us, but by us, by the men and women who are not content to settle for the world as it is, who have the courage to remake the world as it should be.

—Barack Obama

• • •

Duty to country extends far beyond active engagement in our armed forces. Duty should be in the hearts and minds of every American who believes in life, liberty, and the pursuit of happiness. Without duty, there is no freedom. Without freedom, there is no hope. Without hope, all else is lost. Together, we have the strength to sustain the freedoms we hold dearly.

—Gregory E. Sapp

• • •

Aspiration

Fear should not be a reason to abandon all hope. Instead, face fear and allow it to be a positive motivation in your life. Proclaim victory over the "How can I" and declare "When can I." After all, you only live once.
—GREGORY E. SAPP

• • •

Do you think it is a vain hope that one day man will find joy in noble deeds of light and mercy, rather than in the coarse pleasures he indulges in today—gluttony, fornication, ostentation, boasting, and envious vying with his neighbor? I am certain this is not a vain hope and that the day will come soon.
—FYODOR DOSTOYEVSKY, *THE BROTHERS KARAMAZOV*

• • •

[Koudelka] looked back, "You?! I know you! You trust beyond reason!"
[Cordelia] met his eyes steadily, "Yes, it's how I get results beyond hope, as you may recall."
—LOIS MCMASTER BUJOLD, *A CIVIL CAMPAIGN*

• • •

After that, work and hope. But never hope more than you work.
—BERYL MARKHAM, *WEST WITH THE NIGHT*

• • •

When there is no hope, there can be no endeavor.
—SAMUEL JOHNSON, *THE RAMBLER*

• • •

The happy union of these states is a wonder; their constitution
is a miracle; their example the hope of liberty throughout the
world.
—JAMES MADISON

• • •

I hope for nothing. I fear nothing. I am free.
—NIKOS KAZANTZAKIS

• • •

What we hope ever to do with ease, we must first learn to do with diligence.
—SAMUEL JOHNSON

• • •

I hope our wisdom will grow with our power and teach us that the less we use our power the greater it will be.
—THOMAS JEFFERSON

• • •

Hope is the bedrock of this nation; the belief that our destiny will not be written for us, but by us; by all those men and women who are not content to settle for the world as it is; who have courage to remake the world as it should be.
—BARACK OBAMA

• • •

My dream is of a place and a time where America will once again be seen as the last best hope of Earth.
—ABRAHAM LINCOLN

• • •

Israel was not created in order to disappear. . . It is the child of
hope and the home of the brave.
—John F. Kennedy

• • •

I came to New York and in only hours, New York did what it does
to people: awakened the possibilities. Hope breaks out.
—Phillip Roth

• • •

People without hope not only don't write novels, but what is
more to the point, don't read them. They don't take long looks at
anything, because they lack courage.
—Flannery O'Connor

• • •

The fact is that it was Franklin Roosevelt who gave hope to a
nation that was in despair and could have slid into dictatorship.
—Newt Gingrich

• • •

Learn from yesterday, live for today, hope for tomorrow.
—ALBERT EINSTEIN

• • •

Do that which is assigned to you, and you cannot hope too much
or dare too much.
—RALPH WALDO EMERSON

• • •

Hope is what led a band of colonists to rise up against an empire;
what led the greatest of generations to free a continent and heal a
nation. . .
—BARACK OBAMA

• • •

A strong mind always hopes and always has cause to hope.
—THOMAS CARLYLE

• • •

A leader is a dealer in hope.
—NAPOLEON BONAPARTE

• • •

Work without Hope draws nectar in a sieve, and Hope without
an object cannot live.
—SAMUEL TAYLOR COLERIDGE

• • •

Each time a man stands up for an ideal, or acts to improve the
lot of others, or strikes out against injustice, he sends forth a tiny
ripple of hope. . .
—ROBERT F. KENNEDY

• • •

Who dares nothing need hope for nothing.
—FRIEDRICH SCHILLER

• • •

None who have always been free can understand the terrible fascinating power of the hope of freedom to those who are not free.
—PEARL BUCK, WHAT AMERICA MEANS TO ME

• • •

War is just when it is necessary; arms are permissible when there is no hope except in arms.
—NICCOLÓ MACHIAVELLI, THE PRINCE

• • •

Desire and hope will push us toward the future.
—MICHEL DE MONTAIGNE

• • •

8

A Basket of Hopes

Fear less, hope more; Eat less, chew more; Whine less, breathe
more; Talk less, say more; Love more, and all good things will be
yours.
—SWEDISH PROVERB

• • •

Hope is important because it can make the present moment less
difficult to bear. If we believe that tomorrow will be better, we can
bear a hardship today.
—THICH NHAT HANH

• • •

When things are bad, we take comfort in the thought that they could always be worse. And when they are, we find hope in the thought that things are so bad they have to get better.
—MALCOLM FORBES

• • •

Hope is faith holding out its hand in the dark.
—GEORGE ILES

• • •

Hope is the feeling that the feeling you have isn't permanent.
—JEAN KERR

• • •

Hope is the dream of a soul awake.
—FRENCH PROVERB

• • •

Hope is a waking dream.
—ARISTOTLE

• • •

While there's life, there's hope.
—CICERO, *AD ATTICUM*

• • •

The very least you can do in your life is figure out what you hope for. And the most you can do is live inside that hope. Not admire it from a distance, but live right in it, under its roof.
—BARBARA KINGSOLVER, *ANIMAL DREAMS*

• • •

Never deprive someone of hope; it might be all they have.
—H. JACKSON BROWN, JR.

• • •

Hope is necessary in every condition.
—SAMUEL JOHNSON

• • •

Strange as it may seem, I still hope for the best, even though the best, like an interesting piece of mail, so rarely arrives, and even when it does it can be lost so easily.
—LEMONY SNICKET, *THE BEATRICE LETTERS*

• • •

Only in the darkness can you see the stars.
—DR. MARTIN LUTHER KING JR.

• • •

God never slams a door in your face without opening a box of
Girl Scout cookies. . .
—ELIZABETH GILBERT, *EAT, PRAY, LOVE*

• • •

Hope is a verb with its shirtsleeves rolled up.
—DAVID ORR

• • •

Hope itself is like a star—not to be seen in the sunshine of
prosperity, and only to be discovered in the night of adversity.
—CHARLES H. SPURGEON

• • •

Everything that is done in this world is done by hope.
—Dr. Martin Luther King Jr.

• • •

We promise according to our hopes and perform according to our fears.
—François de La Rochefoucauld

• • •

Farewell Hope, and with Hope farewell Fear.
—John Milton, *Paradise Lost*

• • •

Be faithful in small things because it is in them that your strength lies.
—Mother Teresa

• • •

The very existence of libraries affords the best evidence that we
may yet have hope for the future of man.
—T. S. ELIOT

• • •

"You can't eat hope," the woman said.
"You can't eat it, but it sustains you," the colonel replied.
—GABRIEL GARCÍA MÁRQUEZ, *EL CORONEL NO TIENE
QUIEN LE ESCRIBA*

• • •

While the heart beats, hope lingers.
—ALISON CROGGON

• • •

You do not need to know precisely what is happening, or
exactly where it is all going. What you need is to recognize the
possibilities and challenges offered by the present moment, and
to embrace them with courage, faith, and hope.
—THOMAS MERTON

• • •

Hope costs nothing.
—COLETTE

• • •

Sometimes good things fall apart, so better things can fall together.
—JESSICA HOWELL

• • •

The sooner you make a mistake and learn to live with it, the better. You're not responsible for everything. You can't control the way things end up.
—COURTNEY SUMMERS, *CRACKED UP TO BE*

• • •

If it were not for hopes, the heart would break.
—THOMAS FULLER

• • •

"You see, we cannot draw lines and compartments and refuse to budge beyond them. Sometimes you have to use your failures as stepping-stones to success. You have to maintain a fine balance between hope and despair." He paused, considering what he had just said. "Yes," he repeated. "In the end, it's all a question of balance."
—ROHINTON MISTRY, *A FINE BALANCE*

• • •

Hope is not the conviction that something will turn out well, but the certainty that something makes sense, regardless of how it turns out.
—VÁCLAV HAVEL

• • •

No one knows for sure that that tomorrow won't come, but most people assume that tomorrow will still exist as usual. This is Toba's Paradox, which means, hope overcomes doubt.
—TOBA BETA

• • •

At what point do you give up—decide enough is enough? There is only one answer really. Never.
—TABITHA SUZUMA, *FORBIDDEN*

• • •

Hope can get you through anything.
—JAMIE FORD, *HOTEL ON THE CORNER OF BITTER AND SWEET*

• • •

When one door closes, another opens; but we often look so long and so regretfully upon the closed door that we do not see the one which has opened.
—ALEXANDER GRAHAM BELL

• • •

Reader, do you think it is a terrible thing to hope when there is really no reason to hope at all? Or is it (as the soldier said about happiness) something that you might just as well do, since, in the end, it really makes no difference to anyone but you?
—KATE DICAMILLO, *THE TALE OF DESPEREAUX: BEING THE STORY OF A MOUSE, A PRINCESS, SOME SOUP, AND A SPOOL OF THREAD*

• • •

And what is hurt but the repository of hope?
—JOYCE CAROL OATES, *FAITHLESS: TALES OF TRANSGRESSION*

• • •

Now I'm making a decision. I choose life. I shall live because there are a few people I want to stay with for the longest possible time and because I have duties to discharge. It is not my concern whether or not life has meaning. If I am unable to forgive, then I shall try to forget. I shall live by force and cunning.
—TAYEB SALIH, *SEASON OF MIGRATION TO THE NORTH*

• • •

I don't buy the idea of second chances. With hope we make a lot of chances.
—TOBA BETA, *MY ANCESTOR WAS AN ANCIENT ASTRONAUT*

• • •

Beware how you take away hope from another human being.
—OLIVER WENDELL HOLMES SR.

• • •

You don't dare think whole even to yourself the entirety of a dear hope or wish let alone a desperate one else you yourself have doomed it.
—WILLIAM FAULKNER, *INTRUDER IN THE DUST*

• • •

Hope for the best, prepare for the worst.
—CHRIS BRADFORD, *YOUNG SAMURAI: THE RING OF EARTH*

• • •

Hope attracts chances.
—Toba Beta, *My Ancestor Was an Ancient Astronaut*

• • •

Hope is the thing with feathers
That perches in the soul,
And sings the tune without the words,
And never stops at all,

And sweetest in the Gale is heard;
And sore must be the storm
That could abash the little Bird
That kept so many warm.

I've heard it in the chilliest land
And on the strangest Sea;
Yet, never, in Extremity,
It asked a crumb of me.
—Emily Dickinson

• • •

To believe and yet to have no hope is to thirst beside a fountain.
—Ann-Marie MacDonald, *Fall on Your Knees*

● ● ●

Nor dread nor hope attend
A dying animal;
A man awaits his end
Dreading and hoping all.
—W. B. Yeats

● ● ●

In the midst of winter, I find within me the invisible summer. . .
—Leo Tolstoy, *The Kingdom of God is Within You*

● ● ●

Hope can be imagined as a domino effect, a chain reaction, each increment making the next increase more feasible. . . There are moments of fear and doubt that can deflate it.
—JEROME GROOPMAN

• • •

Hope has a cost. Hope is not comfortable or easy. Hope requires personal risk. It is not about the right attitude. Hope is not about peace of mind. Hope is action. Hope is doing something. The more futile, the more useless, the more irrelevant and incomprehensible an act of rebellion is, the vaster and more potent hope becomes.
—CHRIS HEDGES

• • •

Hope is a flicker, a candle flame kept burning by the simple act of breathing.
—JOAN CLARK

• • •

Hope knows no fear.
Hope dares to blossom even inside the abysmal abyss.
Hope secretly feeds and strengthens promise.
—SRI CHINMOY

• • •

I suppose she's right. It's like a metaphor for life: No one wants an ornery old goat, but we can't resist opening the door anyway. We can't keep from hoping.
—LAUREN MYRACLE, *BLISS*

• • •

. . . omniscience about life and death is not within a physician's purview. A doctor should never write off a person a priori.
—JEROME GROOPMAN, *THE ANATOMY OF HOPE: HOW PEOPLE PREVAIL IN THE FACE OF ILLNESS*

• • •

Doubt is the ally of hope, not its enemy, and together they made
all the blessing he had.
—BARRY UNSWORTH, *SACRED HUNGER*

• • •

I am hopeful, though not full of hope, and the only reason I don't
believe in happy endings is because I don't believe in endings.
—EDWARD ABBEY, *POSTCARDS FROM ED: DISPATCHES AND
SALVOS FROM AN AMERICAN ICONOCLAST*

• • •

I had learned that every patient has the right to hope, despite
long odds, and it was my role to help nurture that hope.
—JEROME GROOPMAN

• • •

It is silly not to hope . . . besides I believe it is a sin.
—ERNEST HEMINGWAY, *THE OLD MAN AND THE SEA*

• • •

. . . but I must reluctantly observe that two causes, the abbreviation of time, and the failure of hope, will always tinge with a browner shade the evening of life.
—EDWARD GIBBON, *MEMOIRS OF MY LIFE*

• • •

Hope was always out ahead of fact, possibility obscured the outlines of reality.
—WALLACE STEGNER, *ANGLE OF REPOSE*

• • •

I can't go on, I'll go on.
—SAMUEL BECKETT, *THE UNNAMEABLE*

• • •

Hope, how she had grown to hate the word. It was an insidious seed planted inside a person's soul, surviving covertly on little tending, then flowering so spectacularly that none could help but cherish it.
—KATE MORTON, *THE FORGOTTEN GARDEN*

• • •

Courage is willful hope.
—JOANNA RUSS, *ON STRIKE AGAINST GOD*

• • •

Believe in the hope of your Life Illusion because this is the only
real thing that you possess!
—SORIN CERIN, *WISDOM COLLECTION*

• • •

Our greatest good, and what we least can spare,
Is hope: the last of our evils, fear.
—JOHN ARMSTRONG, *ART OF PRESERVING HEALTH*

• • •

For the hopes of men have been justly called waking dreams.
—BASIL, BISHOP OF CAESAREA

• • •

A Basket of Hopes

Hope! of all ills that men endure,
The only cheap and universal cure.
—ABRAHAM COWLEY, *THE MISTRESS, FOR HOPE*

• • •

You ask what hope is. He [Aristotle] says it is a waking dream.
—DIOGENES

• • •

Hope springs eternal in the human breast;
Man never is, but always to be blest.
—ALEXANDER POPE, *ESSAY ON MAN*

• • •

Hope is being able to see that there is light despite all the
darkness.
—DESMOND TUTU

• • •

Hope is the cordial that keeps life from stagnating.
—Samuel Richardson

• • •

Hope is the best possession.
—William Hazlitt

• • •

False hopes are more dangerous than fears.
—J. R. R. Tolkien, *The Children of Húrin*

• • •

Hope is a good breakfast but it is a bad supper.
—Francis Bacon

• • •

Fear cannot be without hope nor hope without fear.
—SPINOZA

• • •

I am prepared for the worst but hope for the best.
—BENJAMIN DISRAELI

• • •

Nothing can be done without hope and confidence.
—HELEN KELLER

• • •

We must accept finite disappointment but never lose infinite
hope.
—DR. MARTIN LUTHER KING JR.

• • •

I find hope in the darkest of days, and focus in the brightest.
—Dalai Lama XIV

• • •

Three grand essentials to happiness in this life are something to do, something to love, and something to hope for.
—Joseph Addison

• • •

We judge a man's wisdom by his hope.
—Ralph Waldo Emerson

• • •

To the last moment of his breath
On hope the wretch relies;
And e'en the pang preceding death
Bids expectation rise.
—Oliver Goldsmith

• • •

You know nothing about Hope, that immortal, delicious maiden forever courted, forever propitious, whom fools have called deceitful, as if it were Hope that carried the cup of disappointment, whereas it is her deadly enemy, Certainty, whom she only escapes by transformation.
—George Eliot, *Daniel Deronda*

• • •

The Worldly Hope men set their Hearts upon
Turns ashes—or it prospers; and anon,
Like Snow upon the Desert's dusty Face
Lighting a little hour or two—is gone.
—Edward Fitzgerald

• • •

Better hope deferred than none.
—Samuel Beckett

• • •

Hope is itself a species of happiness, and, perhaps, the chief happiness which this world affords: but like all other pleasures immoderately enjoyed, the excesses of hope must be expiated by pain, and the expectations improperly indulged must end in disappointment.
—SAMUEL JOHNSON

• • •

The boldness of the hope men entertain transcends all former experience.
—RALPH WALDO EMERSON

• • •

Be careful what you wish for because you just might get it.
—ANONYMOUS

• • •

We judge a man's wisdom by his hope.
—RALPH WALDO EMERSON

• • •

I just couldn't write anything without hope in it.
—Oscar Hammerstein

• • •

Hope in the face of difficulty. Hope in the face of uncertainty. The audacity of hope.
—Barack Obama

• • •

I give you the mausoleum of all hope and desire. . . I give it to you not that you may remember time but that you might forget it now and then for a moment, and not spend all of your breath trying to conquer it.
—William Faulkner, *The Sound and the Fury*

• • •

Hope bases vast premises upon foolish accidents and reads a word where, in fact, only a scribble exists.
—John Updike, "Pidgeon Feathers"

• • •

Conclusion

We hope these quotations about hope have been able to inspire, intrigue, and even breed caution about what can constitute a hugely life-affirming function of thought.

So often, as in Matthew Arnold's memorable *Dover Beach*, the hope, the expectation, is for an antidote to a world that has proved less than we long thought it should be. It is a stay against chaos and violence. It pleads, in the poem, for something that is possible and practical and not without challenge: That the two lovers be true to one another.

Hope mingles with prayer and a desire for a more rational, thoughtful, wise, spiritual world. It can be quiet or "audacious"— seeking real goals between people close to you or hoping for grand and perhaps radical changes in the ways of the world. We enjoyed collecting these varied and sometimes challenging instances of hope, and hope at least some of them will become part of your life.

Index

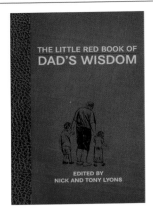

The Little Red Book of Dad's Wisdom

Edited by Nick and Tony Lyons

A collection of more than 270 memorable quotations about the relationships between fathers and their sons and daughters—some wise, some thoughtful, and some downright hilarious. The musings, advice, and observations inside are drawn from famous writers, politicians, actors, comedians, athletes, businessmen, and philosophers. Complete with a new foreword by Nick and Tony Lyons, *The Little Red Book of Dad's Wisdom* is the perfect Father's Day—or any day—gift for dad.

$16.95 Hardcover • ISBN 978-1-61608-244-4

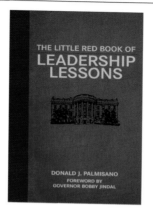

The Little Red Book of Leadership Lessons
by Donald J. Palmisano

Foreword by Governor Bobby Jindal

Anyone can claim to be a leader in times of calm, but crisis situations separate the true visionaries from the false ones. Recent events in global affairs make it increasingly apparent that nations must cultivate and encourage true leaders—and eschew false ones—if they hope to survive.

Fortunately, effective leadership is a skill that can be taught, especially through the study of exemplary figures of the past. Donald J. Palmisano explores the vital qualities that every American should look for in a leader by gleaning lessons from great figures throughout history. Readers will learn about the importance of courage, persistence, decisiveness, and communication as the foundation of a strong leader. *The Little Red Book of Leadership Lessons* provides crucial advice for those who aspire to become effective leaders in any position.

$16.95 Hardcover • ISBN 978-1-62087-191-1

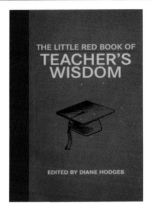

The Little Red Book of Teacher's Wisdom

Edited by Diane Hodges

Known for her motivational and humorous books, Diane Hodges provides the ultimate collection of inspirational quotes and reflective sayings designed to influence, encourage, and motivate educators. Complete with full-color illustrations, these quotes inspire teachers to step outside the guidelines and truly reach their students. The musings, advice, and observations are drawn from famous writers, politicians, scientists, actors, comedians, businessmen, and philosophers. Celebrate the wit, wisdom, and creativity that encompass the world of teaching.

$16.95 Hardcover • ISBN 978-1-61608-607-7

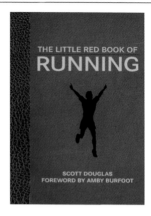

The Little Red Book of Running
by Scott Douglas
Foreword by Amby Burfoot

Scott Douglas offers the advice he's gleaned from three decades of running, from twenty years as a running writer, and from the deep connections he's made with top runners and coaches around the country and around the world. The 250 tips offered here are the next best thing to having a personal coach or an experienced running partner. Douglas includes tips for increasing your daily, weekly, and yearly mileage; advice on increasing your speed and racing faster; useful knowledge on how to stay injury-free and be a healthy runner; and much more.

The range of tips means there's something for every runner. You have the questions: What running apparel is best? What kind of gear do you need to run in the rain or snow? How do you find time in a busy schedule to run? How can you set and achieve meaningful goals? Douglas has the answers.

$16.95 Hardcover • ISBN 978-1-61608-296-3

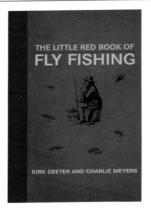

The Little Red Book of Fly Fishing
by Kirk Deeter and Charlie Meyers

Two highly respected outdoor journalists, Kirk Deeter of *Field & Stream* and Charlie Meyers of the *Denver Post*, have cracked open their notebooks and shared advice on the sport of fly fishing, based on a range of new and old experiences—from interviews with the late Lee Wulff to travels with maverick guides in Tierra del Fuego.

The mission of *The Little Red Book of Fly Fishing* is to demystify and uncomplicate the tricks and tips that make a great trout fisher. Conceived in the "take dead aim" spirit of Harvey Penick's classic instructional on golf, *The Little Red Book of Fly Fishing* offers a simple, digestible primer on the basic elements of fly fishing: the cast, presentation, reading water, and selecting flies. In the end, this collection of 240 tips is one of the most insightful, plainly spoken, and entertaining works on this sport—one that will serve both novices and experts alike in helping them reflect and hone their approaches to fly fishing.

$16.95 Hardcover • ISBN 978-1-60239-981-5